Guilty, Guilty, Guilty!

Doonesbury books by G. B. Trudeau

Still a Few Bugs in the System

The President Is a Lot Smarter Than You Think

But This War Had Such Promise

Call Me When You Find America

Guilty, Guilty, Guilty!

Guilty, Guilty, Guilty!

a *Doonesbury* book by G. B. Trudeau

Holt, Rinehart and Winston
New York Chicago San Francisco

To Annie, of course

Published simultaneously in Canada by Holt, Rinehart
and Winston of Canada, Limited
Library of Congress Catalog Card Number: 73-15162
ISBN: 0-03-012511-1
First Edition
Printed in the United States of America: III
The cartoons in this book have appeared in newspapers
in the United States and abroad under the auspices of
Universal Press Syndicate.

HE'S NOT OUT HERE, MIKE!
WELL, TRY THE COFFEE SHOP, ZONKER!
HEY, MIKE, WHO IS THIS GUY YETSKY ANYWAY?
HE'S A POET, BERNIE! YURI YETSKY IS PROBABLY THE MOST FAMOUS RUSSIAN COUNTRY POET LIVING!
HIS AGENT TOLD ME TO MEET YETSKY HERE AT THE STUDENT UNION BEFORE HIS READING... I CAN'T UNDERSTAND WHY HE'S NOT HERE...
HEY, MIKE...
HAMLET
GB Trudeau
...I THINK I'VE FOUND OUR BOY!

LADIES AND GENTS! I AM VERY PLEASED TO PRESENT TO YOU THE GREAT RUSSIAN POET, YURI YETSKY! LET'S HEAR IT!
CLAP! YEA! CLAP!
YEA!
CLAP!
THANK YOU. I TAKE GREAT PLEASURE IN BEING HERE IN AMERICA AGAIN. I GREATLY ADMIRE THE AMERICAN PEOPLE!
ON MY LAST VISIT, I WROTE SCORES OF POEMS ABOUT AMERICA, FROM THE MOMENT I ARRIVED TO THE MOMENT I LEFT. I WOULD LIKE TO SHARE THESE WITH YOU TONIGHT!
ALRIGHT. STARTING WITH NEWARK AIRPORT...

I'D LIKE TO MOVE ON FROM MY AMERICAN POEMS TO THOSE I WROTE IN RUSSIA. THIS FIRST ONE IS ENTITLED "THE RUSSIAN OLYMPIC BASKETBALL TEAM."
BOOO!!
BOO!
BOO!
SSS!
BOO!
I HAD HOPED THIS OCCASION COULD TRANSCEND NATIONALISM. OBVIOUSLY IT WON'T. IT IS WITH GREAT DESPAIR THAT I REFRAIN FROM READING THE OFFENDING POEM!
MY NEXT POEM IS ENTITLED "OLGA AND THE GLORIOUS WOMEN'S GYMNASTICS TEAM FROM THE U.S.S.R."
©B Trudeau

THAT CONCLUDES MY RECITAL. ARE THERE ANY QUESTIONS YOU'D LIKE TO ASK?
YES! MR. YETSKY, WHAT IS "TRUTH"?
THIS QUESTION YOU ASK— IT IS SO MARVELOUS! SUCH A QUESTION FROM ONE SO YOUNG! IT IS FABULOUS!
IN RUSSIA, WE HAVE STUDENTS WHO ASK SUCH QUESTIONS. I AM ALWAYS EXCITED TO SEE THEIR ZEAL, THEIR YOUTHFUL EAGERNESS, THEIR FLASHING INTENSITY!
NEXT QUESTION.

ARE THERE ANY MORE QUESTIONS?
MR. YETSKY, IS IT TRUE YOU WERE ONCE SELF-EFFACING?
DA. I CONFESS THAT WHEN I CAME TO THIS COUNTRY YEARS AGO, MY SPIRIT WAS LACKING IN CONFIDENCE. BUT ONE FALL DAY, AS I DROVE THROUGH MICHIGAN TO A READING IN DETROIT, I WAS BLESSED WITH A VISION!
MY GENIUS CAME TO ME IN A REVELATION! "YETSKY," I SAID, "IT'S TRUE, COMRADE—YOU ARE INDEED THE EXTRAORDINARY MORTAL! YOU ARE... TRUTH!"
WHEN I REACHED DETROIT, I BOUGHT MY SHADES.
GBTrudeau

YOUNG MAN, I WOULD APPRECIATE MY SPEAKER'S FEE BEFORE I LEAVE. MY EXPENSES, UNHAPPILY, HAVE BEEN HIGH.
WHAT? ARE YOU NOT PAID WELL AT HOME?
NO. I ENJOY NO SPECIAL LUXURY. YOU SEE, I AM A POET AND SOCIALIST. ALL MY "POSSESSIONS" ARE SPIRITUAL.
THAT CERTAINLY WASN'T THE IMPRESSION WE GOT WHEN YOU DROVE UP TO THE HALL THIS MORNING.
A TACTLESS REFERENCE TO MY FERRARI, I ASSUME?
WELL... YEAH.
GBTrudeau

YURI, I'M QUITE HONORED THAT YOU CAME ALL THE WAY OVER HERE TO THE COFFEEHOUSE FOR A RAP! I'VE REALLY BEEN LOOKING FORWARD TO MEETING YOU!
YOU OUGHT TO FIND SOME DYNAMITE MATERIAL FOR YOUR POEMS. THERE'S LOTS GOING ON HERE- PEOPLE GETTING INTO EACH OTHER'S HEADS, THAT SORT OF THING!
YOU KNOW, THE KIDS HAVE REALLY DUG YOUR POETRY, YURI. THE WAY THEY TALK, IT SEEMS YOU'RE PRACTICALLY IN THE SAME LEAGUE AS SOME OF OUR BIG BOYS... LIKE ROD McKUEN!
HEY! YOU'VE HEARD OF HIM, HUH?

HMM.. MAIL'S LATE TODAY.
MAILMAN!
WALDEN
ZONKER! HEY, WHAT GIVES, HOMBRE?
OL' RALPHIE'S SICK. I TOLD HIM I'D TAKE OVER FOR HIM THIS WEEK!
WALDEN
U.S.M
OH, HERE'S YOUR MAIL, KID! FRANKLY, I'VE SEEN BETTER. YOUR MOM IS FINE, BUT YOUR DATE'S OFF FOR THIS WEEKEND, AND YOU FAILED ENGLISH!
WELL, SEE YA!
WALDEN
U.S.M
"NEITHER RAIN NOR SNOW NOR SLEET!.."
WALDEN
MAIL

HI, MR. POSTMAN!
'MORNING, KIDLINGS! GOT A PARCEL FOR YOU!
U.S.M
OH, BOY! IS THIS IT?
I DON'T KNOW! THERE'S NO RETURN ADDRESS.
U.S.M
WELL, LOOK AT THE POSTMARK! IS IT... YES!
U.S.
BATTLE CREEK, MICHIGAN!
IT'S OUR TONY-THE-TIGER RAY GUNS!
OH, WOW!
U.S.

IT'S ABOUT TIME YOU GOT HERE, MAILMAN! I'M EXPECTING A LETTER FROM MY DAUGHTER AT WELLESLEY!
U.S.M
SHE'S ONLY A FRESHMAN, BUT SHE'S DOING MIGHTY WELL! MY CATHY IS REALLY SOME-THING SPECIAL!
U.S.
CATHY? SAY, SHE MUST BE THE ONE WHO WROTE YOU THAT SHE'S NOW LIVING WITH A SAXOPHONE PLAYER IN BOSTON!
U.S.
WHAT?!
SURE, CATHY, THAT'S RIGHT!
U.S.

I THINK THIS RAIN, SNOW AND SLEET BUSINESS IS FINALLY GETTING TO ME. I WANT OUT!
MAIL
I DON'T KNOW HOW POSTMEN CAN DO THIS ALL YEAR ROUND. I'VE ONLY BEEN AT IT ONE WEEK AND I'M EXHAUSTED!
AT LEAST I HAVEN'T MET UP WITH ANY FEROCIOUS DOGS! WE ITINERANT PUBLIC SERVANTS ARE TERRIFIED OF POOCHIES!
KNOCK! KNOCK!
MAIL
©BTucker
YEAH?
WHO IS IT, BOY?
MAIL

THE PRESIDENT IS PREPARING TO GIVE HIS SPEECH NOW, HARRY. THE BIG QUESTION IS WILL MR. NIXON CHOOSE HIS GENERATION OF PEACE THEME OR HIS NEW PERMISSIVENESS THEME?..
WELL, HOWARD, AS YOU KNOW, THE PRESIDENT HAS RECENTLY BEEN EXPRESSING SOME INTEREST IN MORAL LEADERSHIP. I'LL SAY HE'LL TRY TO NAIL THIS ONE DOWN...
MY FELLOW HARD-WORKING AND LAW-ABIDING CITIZENS...
YOU CALLED IT, HARRY! HE'S GOING WITH PERMISSIVENESS!
©B Trudeau

DAD? IT'S ME, MARK!
SAY, DAD, I'VE GOT GREAT NEWS! I JUST GOT MY GRADES AND GUESS WHAT? I MADE THE DEAN'S LIST! ISN'T THAT TERRIFIC?
DAD?... DAD?..
DEAR?.. DEAR?..

DEAN'S LIST? INCREDIBLE! YOUR BOY MARK HAS COME A LONG WAY SINCE HIS DAYS ON THE OL' BARRICADES.
YOU BET HE HAS! AND I'VE GOT A FEELING IT'S ONLY A BEGINNING! HE'S GOING TO MAKE THAT DEAN'S LIST AGAIN NEXT TERM!
AND THEN AGAIN! AND THEN GRADUATION WITH PHI BETA KAPPA... AND THEN – DARE I SAY IT?...
LAW SCHOOL?
HEY, WOULDN'T THAT BE SOMETHING?
GBTrudeau

O.K., DEAR, I'LL PUT YOUR WINTER COAT IN THE MAIL FIRST THING TOMORROW.
OH, MARK, YOUR REPORT CARD CAME YESTERDAY. YOUR FATHER RAN RIGHT OUT AND HAD IT FRAMED. HE'S HANGING IT UP IN HIS STUDY NOW.
MARK, DEAR, WHATEVER OTHER SATISFACTIONS YOU MAY DERIVE FROM THIS SCHOLARLY ACHIEVEMENT, I HOPE YOU KNOW YOU'VE MADE YOUR FATHER VERY, VERY HAPPY.
SIGH

MS. CAUCUS, IS MY DADDY A CHAUVINIST PIG?
WELL, I DON'T KNOW, DEAR. WHAT'S YOUR DADDY LIKE?
WELL, HE'S NOT NICE TO MY MOMMY.
HE'S ALWAYS ORDERING HER AROUND, AND THEN AFTER, HE CHUCKS HER UNDER THE CHIN AND SAYS, "YOU LOVE IT, WOMAN, ADMIT IT!"
YOUR DADDY IS A CHAUVINIST PIG.
WELL, I THOUGHT SO...

NO, HONEY, NOTHING'S WRONG. IT'S JUST THAT I'VE BEEN WORKING HARD ALL DAY LONG AND THE FIRST THING YOUR FATHER DOES WHEN HE GETS HOME IS DEMAND THAT HIS DINNER BE ON TIME!
SNIFF
YOU'RE A PIG, DADDY!
HUH?

WHADDA YA MEAN, MY EGGS AREN'T READY!? HOW LONG DOES IT TAKE TO COOK TWO LOUSY EGGS?!
HUH?
I'VE GOT A LONG DAY AHEAD OF ME, SO HURRY UP WITH THOSE EGGS BEFORE I LOSE MY TEMPER!
OINK, OINK.
WHAT DID YOU SAY?!
YOU'RE CUTE WHEN YOU GET MAD, DADDY.

HELLO?.. YES, YES, THIS IS SHE.. YES, MR. ALLEN, WHAT CAN I DO FOR YOU?.. WHAT?
I DON'T KNOW WHAT YOU'RE TALKING ABOUT, MR. ALLEN! I HAVE **NOT** BEEN "FEEDING MARY A LOT OF SUBVERSIVE POPPYCOCK!"
YES, MR. ALLEN, YES, BUT.... WHAT?!..
HAVE YOU **REALLY** BEEN CALLING YOUR FATHER A PIG, DEAR?
UH-HUH.

YOU KNOW HOW THIS WHOLE "PIG" THING STARTED, DON'T YOU? THROUGH YOUR PERMISSIVENESS, THAT'S HOW!
NOW, DEAR...
IT'S TRUE! YOU HAD TO GO SEND MARY TO SOME RADICAL DAY CARE CENTER WHERE SHE PICKED UP THESE IDEAS!
WELL, I'M TELLING YOU SOMETHING, JUDY! SINCE YOU WON'T TAKE A HAND IN GIVING THIS KID A SET OF MORAL IM-PERATIVES, I WILL!
FROM NOW ON, I WANT YOU IN BY TEN!
AW, DADDY!
©BTrudeau

MR. PRESIDENT? SIR, WE SEEM TO BE HAVING MORE PROBLEMS THAN WE EXPECTED GETTING YOUR APPOINTEES CONFIRMED. THE CONGRESS IS GIVING US A HARD TIME!
THE CONGRESS? YOU MEAN THE HOUSE AND THE SENATE?
THAT'S RIGHT, SIR. THE WORD IS THAT THEY RESENT YOUR LACK OF RAPPORT.
THEY CAN'T DO THIS! IT'S IMPORTANT I HAVE MEN I CAN WORK WITH!
SIR, MAYBE YOU BETTER HAVE A LITTLE CHAT WITH SOME CONGRESSIONAL LEADERS...
YOU'RE RIGHT! GET ME MIKE MANFRED ON THE PHONE!
THAT'S "MANSFIELD," SIR...
GBTrudeau

GOOD AFTERNOON, SPORTS FANS, AND WELCOME TO ABC TELEVISION'S "FOOTBALL HIGHLIGHTS OF 1972"! TODAY WE HAVE HERE...
SIR?
MR. PRESIDENT?.. EXCUSE ME, SIR, BUT MR. BREZHNEV IS ON THE LINE. HE WANTS TO DISCUSS A NEW SUMMIT MEETING TO EASE WORLD TENSION..
SIGH
LOOK, COULD YOU ASK HIM TO CALL BACK IN AN HOUR?..
©GBTrudeau

I'M TELLING YOU, DAN, I'VE HAD IT! IF ZIEGLER DOESN'T GIVE US A DECENT BRIEFING TODAY, THEN I'M QUITTING THE WHITE HOUSE PRESS CORPS FOR GOOD!
SSHH.. KEEP IT DOWN!.. HERE HE COMES..
GOOD AFTERNOON, GENTLEMEN!
TODAY THE PRESIDENT HAD LUNCH AT 12:30. LATER, HE MADE MANY IMPORTANT PHONE CALLS!
THANK YOU.
THAT DOES IT!!
GBTrudeau

YOU'RE THE NEW D.J.?
YEAH, ROGER ASKED ME TO DROP BY. WHERE'S THE STUDIO?
NOT SO FAST. YOU GOT ANY EXPERIENCE?
HEY, MAMMAS AND DADDIES! UNWIND YOUR MINDS AND RETHREAD YOUR HEADS! PAPPA SOUL GONNA LAY DOWN SOME RIFFS TO MAKE GROOVIN' BEHOOVIN'!
FIRST DOOR TO YOUR RIGHT.
BEAUTIFUL.
©B Trudeau

HELLO? WBBY REQUEST LINE!
"MARVELOUS MARK?" I'D LIKE TO DEDICATE "BABY BLUE" TO ELMER.
OH? WHY'S THAT, DEAR?
WELL, SEE, I HAD THIS GROOVY GUY WHO WAS REALLY OUTASITE, BUT THEN THE RELATIONSHIP TURNED OUT TO BE A BUMMER...
SEE, HE STARTED DIGGING ANOTHER CHICK. SO I STARTED GOING OUT WITH HIS BEST FRIEND, TO PAY HIM BACK. BUT THE WHOLE THING GOT TOO PHYSICAL, TOO MUCH SEX, YOU KNOW WHAT I MEAN, "MARVELOUS MARK"?
ACTUALLY, "MARVELOUS MARK" IS KINDA SORRY HE ASKED...
SO I TOLD HIM TO BUG OFF, SEE...
©GBTrudeau

O.K., BROTHERS AND SISTERS, DEDICATION TIME! CALL 'EM IN, AND THIS TIME I WANT SOME CLASS DEDICATIONS!
THE ONES YESTERDAY WERE PRETTY BUSH, FOLKS, SO GET IT TOGETHER FOR OL' "MARVELOUS," O.K.?
FROM THE GUYS DOWN AT BARNEY'S BAR AND GRILL, THIS ONE'S GOING OUT TO THE MEMORY OF BERTRAND RUSSELL!
NOW, THAT'S MORE LIKE IT, CAMPERS!
©BTrudeau

"MARVELOUS MARK" REQUEST LINE! MAY I HELP YOU?
HELLO, "MARVELOUS MARK"?.. I'M GOING TO COMMIT SUICIDE.
GEE, I'M SORRY, BUT THIS IS JUST A REQUEST LINE...
YOU DON'T UNDERSTAND! MY BOY-FRIEND LEFT ME, AND I'M GOING TO END IT ALL..
THAT'S TOUGH.. REALLY! BUT I'M TRYING TO DO A SHOW...
I'VE GOT OVER 175 SLEEPING PILLS HERE, AND...
LOOK, HONEY, YOU WANNA DEDICATE A SONG OR NOT?!
"CAN'T LIVE WITHOUT YOU," FROM SHERRY TO ABNER.

HEADS UP, DUDES AND CHICKS! TIME FOR TODAY'S VIETNAM QUICK-QUIZ! HERE'S THE QUESTION! "HOW MANY TONS OF BOMBS WERE DROPPED ON VIETNAM DURING NOVEMBER OF 1972?"
NOW, REMEMBER, THAT'S ABOVE THE 20TH PARALLEL AND EVERYTHING, O.K.? IT'S THE WHOLE WORKS WE'RE AFTER! LET'S PHONE THOSE ANSWERS IN, GANG!
RING!
HELLO, "MARVELOUS MARK" SHOW!.. YES.. YES... YES! 93,470 TONS IS ABSOLUTELY RIGHT!
WE'VE GOT A WINNER!
O.K., CUT TO NEWS.
©BTrudeau

TIME AGAIN FOR THE **WBBY VIETNAM QUICK-QUIZ,** CAMPERS! TODAY'S QUESTION IS, "WHAT HAS BEEN THE EFFECT OF THE WAR ON THE MORAL FIBER OF THE NATION?"
RING!
HELLO! **"MARVELOUS MARK"** SPEAKING! YES... YES... WHAT'S YOUR NAME, DARLIN'?.. SHEILA MOFFIT! FINE!.. HOW OLD ARE YOU, SHEILA?.. TWELVE! GOOD! O.K., GOT AN ANSWER FOR ME?
"THE EFFECT HAS BEEN A DETERIORATION OF SPIRITUAL PRIORITIES" IS **CORRECT!**
YOU ARE TODAY'S WBBY WINNER!
OH, MY! A FREE COPY OF THE PENTAGON PAPERS GOIN' OUT TO SHEILA MOFFIT!
WE'VE GOT A WINNER!
GBTrudeau

MIKE, IT'S INCREDIBLE HOW MANY PEOPLE WHO COME IN HERE ARE TALKING ABOUT MARK'S NEW RADIO SHOW...
I SAW "MARVELOUS" HIMSELF ON THE STREET YESTERDAY. HE TOLD ME HE'S BEEN ENJOYING EVERY MINUTE OF IT...
REALLY?
WELL, ACTUALLY, THERE IS THE PROBLEM OF THE ADS...
THE ADS?
..AND SOAKS UP EXCESS SKIN OIL! TOUGH AGAINST BLACKHEADS, TOO!
©GBTrudeau

HEY, ROGER! BRING ME MY LUNCH! I'VE GOTTA EAT WHILE THE NEWS IS ON!
HERE IT IS, MARK!
QUICK! GIVE IT HERE!
WOW! HURRY UP, MARK! YOU'VE ONLY GOT TEN SECONDS LEFT... SEVEN!.. FIVE... FOUR... TWO, ONE!
©GBTrudeau
YOU'RE ON!
GWOOPY GLOPA MMPH SCHLA!
MMPH...

ZONKER! WHAT ARE YOU DOING HERE?
YOU FORGOT TO GO TO YOUR MATH RETAKE EXAM! NOW YOU'RE GOING TO FAIL FOR SURE!
BUMMER.
©B Trudeau

MIKE, I'VE DECIDED TO WRITE MY POLITICAL SCIENCE PAPER ON VIETNAM...
REALLY?
YEAH. SEE, I THINK IT'S ABOUT TIME SOMEONE PUT TOGETHER A STUDY OF ALL THE POSITIVE REASONS FOR OUR INVOLVEMENT...
I'D LIKE TO PRESENT THE ADMINISTRATION'S POINT OF VIEW IN SOME DETAIL..
HMM... HOW LONG DOES THE PAPER HAVE TO BE?..
TWO PAGES.
SHOULD BE ENOUGH..
©BTrudeau

Thesis proposal.
TAP TAP
In my paper, I intend to outline the major positive aspects of our involvement in Vietnam.
TAP TAP
I will take as comprehensive an approach as possible, but it should be noted there are many problems in writing such a thesis.
TAP TAP
Ridicule and abuse from my friends, to name two.
TAP TAP
©GBTrudeau

PROFESSOR WESTON?
YES?
B.D. HERE, SIR. I JUST WANTED TO GIVE YOU A PROGRESS REPORT ON MY PAPER ON VIETNAM. IT'S COMING ALONG FINE! WOULD YOU LIKE TO HEAR THE FIRST PAGE?
AH... SURE..
"IT IS MY BELIEF THAT LYNDON JOHNSON WILL BE REMEMBERED AS ONE OF THE GREAT ONES. AT A TIME WHEN THE WAR WAS AT ITS MOST UNPOPULAR, MR. JOHNSON SHOWED COURAGE, AUDACITY, AND GREAT LEADER-SHIP.
"IT WOULD BE DIFFICULT NOT TO COMPARE HIM WITH ROGER STAUBACH."
TRY, B.D., TRY!
©GBTrudeau

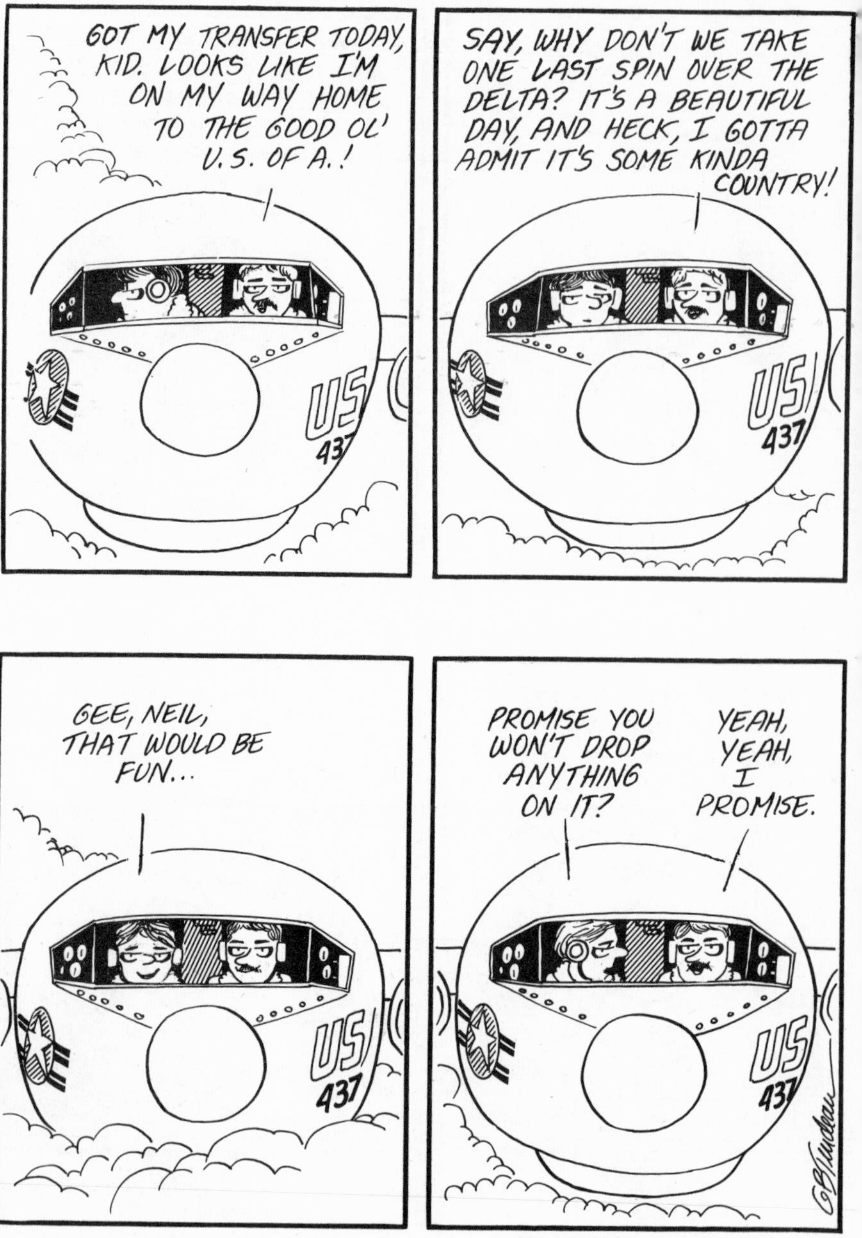
GOT MY TRANSFER TODAY, KID. LOOKS LIKE I'M ON MY WAY HOME TO THE GOOD OL' U.S. OF A.!
SAY, WHY DON'T WE TAKE ONE LAST SPIN OVER THE DELTA? IT'S A BEAUTIFUL DAY, AND HECK, I GOTTA ADMIT IT'S SOME KINDA COUNTRY!
US 437
GEE, NEIL, THAT WOULD BE FUN...
PROMISE YOU WON'T DROP ANYTHING ON IT?
YEAH, YEAH, I PROMISE.
GBTrudeau

I'LL BE DOWNSTAIRS IN A MINUTE, DEAR. I'VE GOT ONE MORE THING TO DO..
WELL, HURRY, DEAR. YOU'RE GOING TO BE LATE FOR YOUR FUND-RAISING TALK TO THE ALUMNI.
THE ALUMNI ARE A ROYAL PAIN IN THE NECK!
O.K., I'M READY...
NOW, DON'T FORGET TO PICK UP THE MILK ON THE WAY HOME...

HOLY MOSES, WILL YOU LOOK AT ALL THOSE INSIPID FACES?! THE THINGS I HAVE TO DO TO KEEP MY UNIVERSITY RUNNING!
GOOD AFTERNOON, FELLOW ALUMNI. IT IS A PLEASURE TO ADDRESS THIS WONDERFULLY DIVERSE GROUP! THERE ARE MANY KINDS OF ALUMNI PRESENT – TALL ONES, SHORT ONES – BUT YOU DO SHARE ONE THING IN COMMON.
MONEY.
A DEEP RESPECT FOR THE FUTURE OF HIGHER EDUCATION!
GBTrudeau

MY FELLOW ALUMNI, THE FINANCIAL SITUATION AT THE UNIVERSITY IS GRAVE. WE MUST HAVE YOUR SUPPORT IF WE ARE TO MAINTAIN OUR STANDARDS OF EXCELLENCE.
SO, LADIES AND GENTLEMEN, I OPEN UP THE FLOOR TO YOUR PLEDGES. HOW MUCH DO I HEAR FOR THE FUTURE OF HIGHER EDUCATION IN AMERICA?!
GOING ONCE, GOING TWICE...
©GBTrudeau

GIVE THE UNIVERSITY A SMALL CHECK? NO, SIR, NOT I! I HAVE NOTED WITH GREAT ALARM YOUR RADICAL APPROACH TO EDUCATION, AND I REFUSE TO SUPPORT IT!
OH, WELL, I GUESS THAT'S THE WAY IT GOES... SAY, I UNDERSTAND YOU HAVE A SON APPLYING FOR ADMISSION NEXT FALL.
HE'LL GET A NICE ROOM, WON'T HE?
I CAN'T PROMISE YOU ANYTHING.
©B Trudeau

NOW, MR. VAN HADEN, AS I UNDERSTAND IT, YOU'RE INTERESTED IN CONTRIBUTING A SUBSTANTIAL GIFT TO THE UNIVERSITY..
CORRECT! I WANT TO GIVE A GYM!
WELL, SIR, WE ALREADY HAVE A FINE GYM. WE ARE, HOW-EVER, IN NEED OF FUNDS FOR NEW PROGRAMS OF STUDY.
NOW LISTEN HERE, YOUNG MAN..
JUST LEAVE IT TO ME, SIR! BELIEVE ME, YOUR MONEY WILL BE WISELY SPENT!
I WANNA GIVE A GYM!
I'LL JUST PUT YOU DOWN FOR THE NEW AFRO-AMERICAN STUDIES PROGRAM..
GBTrudeau

HEY! A LETTER FROM PHRED! IT'S ABOUT TIME!
WALDEN
"DEAR RUNNING DOG: PLEASE FORGIVE MY DELINQUENCY IN NOT WRITING YOU SOONER. I HAVE BEEN TRÉS BUSY.
WALDEN
"RIGHT AFTER THE CEASE-FIRE, I SHED MY WICKED WAYS AND OPENED UP THE DELTA'S FIRST SOUVENIR SHOP."
NO!
WALDEN
NINE BUCKS?!
LOOK, MAN, I GOT A FAMILY TO FEED!
POSTCARDS $1.00
Mekong Delta
Hats

DON'T BE LONG, ELLEN! THE BUS LEAVES FOR HUÉ IN TEN MINUTES!
POSTCARDS $1.00
HATS $5.00
HEE HEE! JUST SHOWIN' THE MISSUS THE DELTA! I USED TO BE STATIONED HERE!
HEY! ME, TOO. I WAS A VIET CONG!
POSTCARDS $1.00
HATS $6.00
REALLY? YOU WERE WORKIN' THIS TURF?
SURE! REMEMBER THAT BIG PRE-DAWN MORTAR ATTACK LAST MAY?
©BTrudeau
POSTCARDS $1.00
HATS $7.00
THAT WAS YOU?!
WELL, MY UNIT!
POSTCARDS $1.00
HATS $8.00

ELLEN, I'D LIKE YOU TO MEET PHRED. HE USED TO BE ONE OF THE ENEMY.
HI YA, MA'AM.
POSTCARDS $1.00
HATS $5.00
I'M PLEASED TO MEET YOU, PHRED. MY HUSBAND HAS TOLD ME SO MUCH ABOUT YOU VIET CONG!
NOTHING BAD, I HOPE.
POSTCARDS $1.00
HATS $6.00
HEE-HEE! NO, NO!... WELL, WE BETTER BE GETTING BACK TO THE BUS. IT'S BEEN NICE TALKING TO YOU..
POSTCARDS $1.00
HATS $7.00
AND IF YOU'RE EVER IN SIOUX FALLS...
RIGHT. THANKS. I WILL.
POSTCARDS $1.00
HATS $8.00
©BTrudeau

BLAM!!
POW!
POW!
RAT-A-TAT-TAT!!
STOP IT, STOP IT, STOP IT!
SORRY ABOUT THE DAMAGE TO YOUR SHOP, CITIZEN!
SORRY?! DON'T YOU KNOW THERE'S A CEASE-FIRE GOING ON?! YOU'RE SCARING OFF MY BUSINESS!
LOOK, WE'RE SORRY! I'LL GIVE YOU A PERSONAL CHECK TO COVER THE DAMAGE..
I DON'T KNOW WHAT'S THE MATTER WITH YOU PEOPLE! FIGHT, FIGHT, FIGHT! THAT'S ALL YOU EVER...
O.K., MOVE OUT, MEN!
HOLD IT, I'VE GOTTA CLEAR THIS WITH THE BANK!
GBTrudeau

HEY, YOU'RE NEW IN THIS CLASS, AREN'T YOU?
THAT'S RIGHT. MY NAME'S SKIP WILLIS. I'M A FRESHMAN.
FRESHMAN? YOU LOOK KINDA OLD TO BE A FRESHMAN.
WELL, I'M TWENTY-SIX. I'M STARTING A LITTLE LATE BECAUSE I SPENT THE LAST SEVEN YEARS IN A P.O.W. CAMP.
WHAT?! A P.O.W.?! IN MY CLASS? YOU'RE KIDDING!
DID SOMEONE SAY A P.O.W.?
SSSHH.. PLEASE..
STOP THE LECTURE!!
HEY! LOOK! HERE HE IS!
WOW!

HI, MIKE, WHO'S THIS?
JOANIE, THIS HERE IS SKIP! WE MET HIM IN CLASS TODAY. HE'S A FORMER P.O.W.!
OH, REALLY? WELL, I'M GLAD TO MEET YOU, SKIP.
I'M GLAD TO MEET YOU JOANIE. WHAT DO YOU DO HERE, THE HOUSEWORK AND STUFF?
DID I SAY SOME THING WRONG?
YEAH, SORT OF..
GBTrudeau

SKIPPER, WHEN YOU WERE LOCKED UP ALL THOSE YEARS, WHAT WAS IT YOU MISSED THE MOST?
THAT'S PRETTY DIFFICULT TO SAY, ZONKER. I MEAN, WE DIDN'T HAVE ANY OF THE THINGS PEOPLE TOOK FOR GRANTED AT HOME..
BUT I GUESS MORE THAN ANYTHING ELSE WHAT I WANTED MOST WAS AN ABSENTEE BALLOT!
WHAT?
DEMOCRACY, FELLAHS, I MISSED DEMOCRACY!
HEY, SO DID WE!

HEY, MIKE! DO YOU HAVE A COPY OF "LIFE" AROUND?
"LIFE"? IT WENT OUT OF BUSINESS, SKIP.
IT WENT OUT OF BUSINESS?!
YUP. FOLDED LAST WINTER!
OH, NO! IT CAN'T HAVE FOLDED! FOR SEVEN YEARS I'VE BEEN LOOKING FORWARD TO SEEING IT AGAIN! I USED TO READ "LIFE" EVERY SUNDAY EVENING!...
OH WELL, NO MATTER! IT'S ABOUT TIME FOR "THE ED SULLIVAN SHOW" ANYWAY!
GB Trudeau

SKIP, WHEN YOU WERE A P.O.W., WERE YOU TREATED PRETTY WELL?
ACTUALLY, MIKE, THAT'S KIND OF A PAINFUL SUBJECT FOR ME...
OH, GEE, I'M SORRY, SKIP, OF COURSE IT IS! THAT WAS VERY INSENSITIVE OF ME. I'M SURE YOU JUST WANT TO FORGET.
WHAT, THEY BEAT YOU OR SOMETHIN'?
B.D.!

..ANYWAY, SO THAT'S THE PRIMARY RAISON D'ÊTRE FOR MY OL' PUDDLE...
HEY, SKIPPER, DON'T LISSEN TO HIM... HE'S JUST MOUTHIN' OFF NONSENSE.
I DON'T THINK SO, B.D. I MEAN, I DON'T ALWAYS UNDERSTAND ZONKER EITHER, BUT IT'S INTERESTING TO GET A FRESH PERSPECTIVE.
AS A MATTER OF FACT, I THINK IT'S THE FREE-THINKERS LIKE ZONKER WHO GIVE THE REST OF SOCIETY A BASIS FOR SOME KIND OF HOPE AND FAITH IN THE FUTURE.
HOW PERCEPTIVE!!
YEECH!
©GBTrudeau

HEY, MIKE, BEFORE I GO, I WANT YOU TO TELL ME WHAT YOU THINK OF MY NEW SERUM.
LATER, BERNIE, I GOTTA RUN THROUGH THESE TESTS..
AW, C'MON, IT'LL ONLY TAKE A SECOND. JUST GIVE ME A QUICK REACTION AND I'LL BE OFF!
O.K., O.K., LET'S SEE..
WELL?
I LOVE IT.
HEE HEE! SEE YA TOMORROW.
RIGHT.
POOF!
GBTrudeau

SAY, SKIP, HAVE YOU MET BERNIE YET?
NO. MIKE TOLD ME ABOUT HIM, THOUGH. HE'S INTERESTED IN SCIENCES, RIGHT?
THAT'S RIGHT. HE SPECIALIZES IN WHAT HE CALLS "MOLECULAR TRANSFORMATION."
HE'S ALWAYS TURNING HIMSELF INTO WEIRD CREATURES - LAST YEAR IT WAS WEREWOLVES, BUT THIS YEAR HE AND MIKE ARE TESTING SOME NEW VARIATIONS.
O.K., NOW WHAT?
BREATHE IN. DEEPER.
©BTrudeau

MIKE! JUST WHAT DO YOU THINK YOU'RE DOING?
HUH?
YOU'RE SUPPOSED TO BE DISSECTING THAT FROG, NOT CUTTING HIM UP INTO LITTLE PIECES!
THOSE AREN'T SUCH LITTLE...
WHEN I ASKED TO HAVE YOU AS MY LAB PARTNER, I THOUGHT YOU WOULD SHOW SOME KIND OF RESPECT FOR YOUR MATERIALS!!
BUT I'M DOING THE BEST I CAN..
BUTCHER.
LOOK, YOU WANT ME TO TRANSFER OUT OR SOMETHING?
©BTrudeau

WHAT IS IT, JOHN?
MR. PRESIDENT, MR. DUC THO IS ON THE PHONE FOR YOU, SIR..
HELLO, LE?.. WHAT CAN I DO FOR YOU?...YES, I'M SORRY ABOUT THE AID, BUT CONGRESS HAS TO ACT ON THAT.. NO, WE HAVEN'T GONE BACK ON OUR PLEDGE... YES, I KNOW ABOUT YOUR SCHOOLS AND HOSPITALS...BUT.. ..BUT..
LOOK, DUC THO, I NEVER PROMISED YOU A ROSE GARDEN!
HEE HEE, HEE!
HA, HA, HA! VERY GOOD, SIR!
GBTrudeau

WELL, I GUESS IT'S ABOUT TIME I GOT THIS OVER WITH. I'VE PUT IT OFF TOO LONG AS IT IS..
HELLO?.. OH, HI, HONEY! IT'S MOMMY. HOW ARE YOU? TERRIFIC!.. WHAT?.. AN "A" IN READING?.. THAT'S GREAT... AND A "B+" IN SPELLING! IMAGINE!
THE ZOO?.. REALLY, WAS THAT FUN?.. YES, THE MONKEYS ARE MY FAVORITES, TOO... YES, AND THE ZEBRAS... SAY, HONEY, IS DADDY HOME?.. FINE.. YES, I'LL HANG ON..
©GBTrudeau
CLINT? HI, I WANT A DIVORCE.

ATE 31
HI, CLINT! THANKS FOR COMING OUT TO MEET ME.
WELL, IT WAS KIND OF A PAIN. TONIGHT IS MY BOWLING NIGHT.
ATE 31
ATE 31
YOU'RE SUCH AN AWFUL PERSON! I CAN'T WAIT TO DIVORCE YOU!
GBTrudeau
ATE 31
HEY, KEEP IT DOWN, WILLYA?
C'MON, LET'S GET IT OVER WITH!

JOANIE,.. I'VE.. AH.. BEEN THINKING ABOUT THIS WHOLE THING.. AND I'D LIKE YOU TO... UM.. YOU KNOW..,LIKE MAYBE WE COULD.. AH.. LIKE WORK SOMETHING...
IOUM
C'MON, CLINT, WHAT IS IT?
OH, FUDGE! I GUESS WHAT I'M TRYING TO SAY IS THAT I WANT YOU TO SIGN UP FOR ANOTHER HITCH!
IOUM
IOUM
YOU ALWAYS WERE GOOD WITH WORDS, CLINT.
©BTrudeau
IOUM

JOANIE, WHILE YOU WERE AWAY, I STARTED TO THINK OUT SOME OF THIS WOMEN'S MOVEMENT STUFF OF YOURS..
YOU'RE OBVIOUSLY VERY BIG ON IT, SO I FIGURED IT MIGHT SAVE OUR MARRIAGE IF I LOOKED INTO IT. WELL, I'M GLAD I DID, BECAUSE I NOW THINK A COMPROMISE IS IN ORDER!
YOU DO?
YES, I DO! I'VE DECIDED THAT IF YOU'D RATHER GO WITHOUT A BRASSIERE, THAT'S FINE WITH ME!
OH, CLINT..
LOOK, I'M MEETIN' YOU HALF-WAY, AREN'T I?!
GBTrudeau

JOANIE?
GOOD NIGHT, CLINTON! I'M SORRY, BUT I WANT TO GO TO BED!
JOANIE, HAVEN'T YOU HEARD A WORD I'VE SAID? I'M TRYING TO TELL YOU.. I'VE MISSED HAVING YOU AROUND!
IN WHAT WAY?
WELL, FOR ONE THING, JOANIE, I'VE MISSED YOUR GREAT CHEESE-BURGERS!
AND YOUR FRIES! I'VE REALLY MISSED YOUR FRIES!
SEE YOU IN COURT.
©GBTrudeau

'MORNING, FOLKS! WHERE'S YOUR ATTORNEY?
ATTORNEY? WE DON'T NEED AN ATTORNEY.
OF COURSE YOU NEED AN ATTORNEY! MURDER IS A PRETTY SERIOUS CHARGE!
MURDER? WHAT ARE YOU TALKING ABOUT? THIS IS A DIVORCE CASE!
DIVORCE CASE?! BUT IT'S RIGHT HERE WRITTEN IN MY APPOINTMENT BOOK! "10:00 A.M. – THE DENVER AX MURDERS TRIAL!"
I GOTTA GET A NEW SECRETARY..
WE COULD COME BACK TOMORROW..
©B'Trudeau

WELL, LET'S GET TO THE HEART OF THE MATTER, SHALL WE? ALIMONY! WHAT'S THE DEAL THERE?
WELL, YOUR HONOR, THERE'S REALLY NOTHING TO DISCUSS. I HAVE NO INTENTION OF ACCEPTING ANY ALIMONY AT ALL FROM CLINTON.
WHA.?
YIPPEE!!
YOU IS WEIRD, HONEY.

JOANIE, I HAVE SOMETHING I WANT YOU TO TAKE WITH YOU...
IT'S A SNAPSHOT OF US THE NIGHT WE GOT ENGAGED. I KNOW WE'RE OFFICIALLY DIVORCED NOW, BUT THERE MIGHT COME A DAY WHEN YOU'LL WANT TO REMEMBER OUR MOMENTS OF HAPPINESS.
GEE, I'M SORRY, CLINTON, MY SUITCASE IS FULL TO THE BRIM. THERE JUST ISN'T ENOUGH ROOM!
FOR A THREE-INCH PHOTO-GRAPH?!
OOP! SEE, IT JUST BARELY CLOSES!
©B.Trudeau

ATE 18
JOANIE, I HOPE YOU'RE SATISFIED – YOU'RE LEAVING A BROKEN MAN BEHIND YOU TONIGHT.
TE 18
IF YOU DON'T MIND, I THINK I'LL GO NOW.. I WANT TO BE BY MYSELF.. ALONE.. YES, I THINK I'LL TAKE A LONG WALK... TO SORT THINGS OUT...
TE 18
OH, COME OFF IT, CLINT, YOU'RE NOT GOING TO DO ANYTHING OF THE SORT! YOU'VE GOT YOUR BOWLING SHOES ON!
TE 18
DO I? OH, YES, SO I DO..
ADIOS!
©BTrudeau

I'M GLAD YOU'RE SPENDING YOUR READING PERIOD WITH US, B.D. IT'S REAL FUN HAVING YOU HOME!
WELL, WALDEN WAS BEGINNING TO GET TO ME.. SAY, WHAT'S FOR DINNER, MOM?
NOTHING.
HUH? WHAT DO YOU MEAN NOTHING?
I'M SORRY, DEAR, WE JUST CAN'T AFFORD DINNER ANYMORE. YOUR FATHER SAYS IT'S A LUXURY!
GBTrudeau
DAD!!
NOW, DEAR, IT'S NOT HIS FAULT..

GOOD MORNING, MR. SCHMIDT. I'D LIKE TO ORDER A QUARTER POUND OF GROUND ROUND, PLEASE.
Special GROUND BEEF $2.50 lb.
EXTR STAM
OH, HEY, GEE, WHY DON'T YOU MAKE THAT A HALF POUND! MY MAN'LL BE HUNGRY TONIGHT!
GOOD IDEA!
NO! WAIT A MINUTE! MAKE THAT A POUND! AND A SLICE OF BOLOGNA!.. AND BACON! GIVE ME TWO BEAUTIFUL STRIPS OF BACON!
CAUTION TO THE WIND, EH, MR. SCHMIDT?
BON APPÉTIT, MADAME!
EXTRA STAMP

DEAR, IT WAS THE BEST PRICE IN TOWN..
$39.40? THAT'S GRAND LARCENY!
BUT MEAT'S EXPENSIVE, AND.. HEY, WHAT ARE YOU GOING TO DO?
I'M GOING DOWNTOWN TO GIVE THAT BANDIT A PIECE OF MY MIND!
WELL, TELL HIM YOU'RE COMING FIRST. DON'T JUST BARGE INTO THE STORE!
DON'T WORRY..
HELLO? I'D LIKE TO MAKE AN APPOINTMENT WITH THE MEAT SURGEON PLEASE.
GBTrudeau

GOOD MORNING, SCHMIDT. MY WIFE PHONED IN AN ORDER EARLIER TODAY.
YES, I'VE GOT IT READY.
Special GROUND BEEF $3.00 lb
EXTRA STAM
HOPE YOU ENJOY THE ROAST. CUT IT FRESH THIS MORNING. THE RECEIPT'S ON THE TOP OF THE BAG THERE.
MR. TAYLOR HERE IS FROM THE FIRST CITY BANK, SCHMIDT. HE'S GIVING ME A MEAT LOAN.
WELL, LET ME JUST TAKE A LOOK AT IT..
HMM.. YES, YES! I THINK WE CAN OFFER YOU SOME VERY ATTRACTIVE TERMS!
OH, GOOD, GOOD!
GB Trudeau

HI, MR. SCHMIDT. GOT MOM'S HAMBURGER ORDER READY?
SURE, B.D.
Special GROUND BEEF $4.00 lb.
EXTRA STAMP
MAN, YOU SHOULD SEE THE LADIES PICKETING YOUR STORE, MR. SCHMIDT.
DON'T REMIND ME.
Special GROUND BEEF $4.00 lb.
EXTRA STAMP
WELL, I JUST WANT YOU TO KNOW I SUPPORT YOU. I REALIZE YOU'RE JUST TRYING TO MAKE ENDS MEET.
WELL, I APPRECIATE THAT, B.D.. YOUR ORDER COMES TO $17.53.
Special GROUND BEEF $4.00 lb.
EXTRA STAMP
THAT'S OUTRAGEOUS!
CHARGE AS USUAL?
Special GROUND BEEF $4.00 lb.
EXTRA STAMP
© G.B. Trudeau

MR. SCHMIDT, I HOPE YOU'LL FORGIVE THE RECENT BEHAVIOR OF MY HUSBAND AND SON. IT'S JUST THAT WE'RE ALL A BIT CONCERNED ABOUT THE COST AND QUALITY OF YOUR MEAT.
Special GROUND BEEF $4.50 lb
EXTRA STAMPS
I SYMPATHIZE, MA'AM, BUT I CAN'T CONTROL THE PRICES. AS FOR THE QUALITY, IT'S EXCELLENT! AS YOU KNOW, I PACK MY OWN MEAT OUT BACK, AND I SELL NOTHING BUT THE BEST BEEF!
Special GROUND BEEF $4.50 lb
EXTRA STAMPS
NEIGH! NEIGH!
Special GROUND BEEF $4.50 lb
EXTRA STAMPS
SAY, HONEY, YOU WANNA TURN DOWN THAT COWBOY MOVIE ON T.V., PLEASE?!
Special GROUND BEEF $4.50 lb
EXTRA STAMPS
GBTrudeau

HEY, WHERE'S OL' MARCUS TODAY? I THOUGHT HE WAS COMING OUT FOR AN AFTER-NOON DIP!
NOPE. HE HAD TO GO BARTEND TODAY AT THE REUNIONS.
BARTEND?
YEAH. HE WANTED TO WORK FOR ONE OF THE MORE RECENT CLASSES, BUT HE GOT STUCK WITH THE CLASS OF '43.
OH, NO!
43
AND DON'T GET ANY HAIR IN MY COCKTAIL, KID!
YESSIR.
GBTrudeau

SO HOW HAVE YOU BEEN, DANNY? GOSH, YOU LOOK WONDERFUL, KID!
CAN'T COMPLAIN, OL' BUDDY. I'VE NEVER FELT FITTER!
HOW ABOUT SUCCESS? HAVE YOU SCORED WELL IN THE SUCCESS CATEGORY?
WELL.. SINCE YOU ASK..
"b. NYC, AUG. 27, 1920; M.A., N.Y.U., 1945; m. RUTH LANE, JUNE 24, 1947; ASST. GEN. MGR. SHERWIN CHEM. 1947-1953; V.P. 1953-1955; CHMN. 1963- ; NAT. CHMN. UNITED FUND 1961-62; CLUBS: MET.; BATH AND TENNIS."
YOU MADE "WHO'S WHO"!!
CERTAINEMENT.
G.B. Trudeau

...AFTER THAT, I JOINED MERRILL FUNDS, AND IT'S BEEN GRAVY EVER SINCE! ...BUT, HOWIE.. HOW ABOUT YOU? WHAT HAVE YOU BEEN UP TO ALL THESE YEARS?
43
ME?.. OH, I STILL HAVEN'T MADE UP MY MIND WHAT I WANT TO DO YET.
HEE HEE! HEE!
AND WHAT'S SO FUNNY ABOUT THAT, MAY I ASK?!
43
HOWIE, THIS IS OUR THIRTIETH REUNION.
I JUST DON'T WANT TO RUSH INTO ANYTHING!..
GBTrudeau

HOWIE, PERHAPS IT'S NONE OF MY BUSINESS, BUT DON'T YOU THINK IT'S ABOUT TIME YOU STARTED LOOKING FOR A JOB?
I MEAN, A MAN'S GOT TO HAVE SOME LIFE'S WORK. UNLIKE MOST OF YOUR CLASSMATES, HOWIE, YOU'VE JUST WASTED YOUR LIFE AWAY!
NONSENSE!
IN THE LAST THIRTY YEARS, I HAVE WATCHED THOUSANDS OF SUNSETS; I'VE PAINTED STILL-LIFES OF FERNS AND INDIAN CORN; I'VE READ THE VERSES OF MILTON, AND I'VE TAKEN LONG WALKS IN THE BERKSHIRES! WHAT HAVE YOU DONE THAT WAS SO GREAT?
WHY, HOWARD, YOU OL' HIPPY, YOU.
DAMN STRAIGHT!

SAY, FRANKIE, WHAT LINE DID YOU FINALLY END UP IN?
WELL, I'VE BEEN WORKING MOSTLY IN DRUGS.
OH? YOU'RE IN PHARMACEUTICS?
NOPE. I DEAL. IT'S NOT SO GREAT FROM A MORAL POINT OF VIEW, BUT TERRIFIC FINANCIALLY.
I REMEMBER HOW YOU GUYS AT BETA ALWAYS SAID I'D BE A SHARP OPERATOR. I THOUGHT ABOUT THAT THE NIGHT I MADE MY FIRST SCORE. WHAT IRONY!
BUT ENOUGH ABOUT ME! HOW'S GINNY AND THE KIDS?!
©BTrudeau

BOOM!
YOU KNOW, IF I DIDN'T KNOW BETTER, I'D SAY THIS WAR HAS STARTED UP AGAIN.
RAT A TAT TAT TAT!
POW!
SPECIAL DELIVERY FOR YOU, PHRED!
IT'S BAD NEWS, I KNOW IT!
V.P.D.
WANT ME TO READ IT TO YOU?
PLEASE.
"GREETINGS.."
I KNEW IT.
©B Trudeau

I DON'T GET IT! WHY AM I BEING DRAFTED? I WAS JUST BEGINNING TO ADJUST TO CIVILIAN LIFE! I THOUGHT WE WERE AT PEACE!
THE IMPERIALIST WARMONGER THIEU HAS VICIOUSLY VIOLATED THE ACCORDS! THE TRUE VIETNAMESE PEOPLE'S GOVERNMENT IS RESPONDING TO THE AGGRESSION OF THE RUNNING DOGS!
OH.. I SEE...
MAN! I'D FORGOTTEN WE TALKED LIKE THAT.

LIEUTENANT, YOU KNOW AS WELL AS I DO THAT IN ORDER TO REACTIVATE ME, YOU'VE GOT TO RENEW MY CONTRACT! AND I'M TELLING YOU, I'M DESERVING OF BETTER TERMS.
MUST I REMIND YOU I'M THE TOP TERRORIST IN THE WHOLE PROVINCE?
LOOK, PHRED, YOU'RE GOOD, I AGREE, BUT YOU'VE GOT TO UNDERSTAND-YOU'RE PRICING YOURSELF RIGHT OUT OF THE WAR!
LOOK, LIEUTENANT, I CAN'T ARGUE ALL DAY. I'VE GOT TO KNOW TODAY WHETHER THE COLONEL ACCEPTS MY TERMS OR NOT- TODAY!
I'LL DO THE BEST I CAN.
SEE, I'M DUE TO GO ON A HOLIDAY SOON. SURFING, YOU UNDERSTAND..
YOU'LL BE HEARING FROM US!
© GBTrudeau

MOM, WHEN MY NEW CONTRACT GOES THROUGH, WE'LL BE SITTING MIGHTY PRETTY! MIGHT EVEN BE ABLE TO GET YOU A NEW MOTORCYCLE.
HEY! VOILÀ! THEY MUST HAVE ACCEPTED MY TERMS ALREADY!
RING! RING!
HELLO? YES, THIS IS HE... WHAT'S THE OFFER?. HUH?
WHAT?!
I'VE BEEN TRADED TO LAOS.
G B Trudeau

I CAN'T BELIEVE IT! I'VE BEEN TRADED TO THE PATHET LAO!
THOSE MONSTERS! THOSE RATS! THEY PUT ME ON WAIVERS, MOM – WITHOUT EVEN TELLING ME! AND NOW I'VE GOT TO PACK UP AND MOVE TO THE STICKS!
SIGH
THEY SAY IT'S VERY LOVELY ON THE PLAIN OF JARS THIS TIME OF YEAR..
©BTrudeau

RON, DOES THE PRESIDENT HAVE ANY COMMENT ON THE MOST RECENT DISCLOSURES IN THE WATERGATE CASE!
NO!
WATERGATE! WATERGATE! WHAT IS THE MATTER WITH YOU GUYS?! WHAT IS THIS SENSELESS ORGY OF RECRIMINATION WEEK AFTER WEEK?!
I'VE ALREADY SAID ALL THAT I'M GOING TO! SO WHY DON'T YOU STOP WASTING BOTH OUR TIME AND ASK ME QUESTIONS I CAN DEAL WITH?
RON, WHAT COLOR SHIRT IS THE PRESIDENT WEARING TODAY?
THAT'S BETTER. BLUE.
GBTrudeau

WHY, HELLO, PAT! WHAT A NICE SURPRISE!
GOOD MORNING, DEAR, I JUST POPPED IN TO SEE IF THE MAIL IS RUNNING ANY BETTER.
I'M AFRAID IT'S NOT, PAT. IT WOULD SEEM THE AMERICAN PEOPLE ARE STILL A LITTLE DISAPPOINTED IN THE WAY I'VE HANDLED THIS WHOLE AFFAIR.
BUT DON'T YOU WORRY, PAT! I'LL REGAIN THEIR FULL TRUST AND RESPECT! ONE WAY OR THE OTHER, I'LL MAKE IT UP TO THEM!
I'LL LOWER MEAT PRICES OR SOMETHING...
THAT WOULD BE A NICE GESTURE, DEAR.

MR. PRESIDENT, THE PRESS IS STILL GIVING RON A PRETTY HARD TIME. THERE'S EVEN MORE CLAMORING FOR DETAILS ON WATERGATE.
YES, YES, I KNOW! I TALKED WITH HIM AGAIN THIS AFTERNOON. WE'RE JUST GOING TO HAVE TO KEEP RIDING IT OUT..
BAH! I CAN'T BELIEVE I'M STILL WASTING MY DAYS WORRYING ABOUT THIS THING!
AND ONLY 1337 LEFT, SIR.
OH, SHUT UP!
©GB Trudeau

NICHOLE, HAVE YOU HEARD ABOUT MARK'S NEW SERIES OF PROFILES ON HIS RADIO SHOW?
NO. WHAT'S IT ON?
THE WATERGATE CONSPIRATORS. HE'S WORKED OUT COMPLETE BIOGRAPHIES ON ALL OF THEM.
BOY, I'LL BET THEY'RE JUST **BRUTAL!**
NOT AT ALL. I READ THEM LAST NIGHT. SOME OF THEM ARE QUITE SENSITIVE.
"LOS ANGELES IS A LONELY TOWN TO GROW UP IN, ESPECIALLY IF YOU'RE A SMALL BOY NAMED H.R. HALDEMAN."

HOW'D YOU LIKE MY PROFILE OF HALDEMAN YESTERDAY, B.D.?
I DIDN'T! YOU MADE IT SOUND LIKE HE WAS COMPLETELY UNFIT FOR HIS JOB FROM THE START!
BUT IT'S TRUE! HAVE YOU ANY IDEA WHAT H.R. WAS BEFORE HE BECAME ONE OF THE MOST POWERFUL MEN ALIVE?
SURPRISE ME!
AN ADVERTISING EXECUTIVE! WITH ABSOLUTELY NO EXPERIENCE IN GOVERNMENT!
SO WHAT?! WHAT DOES THAT PROVE?!
HOW DO YOU KNOW HE DIDN'T DO A LOT OF READING UP ON HIS OWN?!
©GBTrudeau

OKAY, STAFF, NOW'S THE TIME FOR US TO DO SOMETHING ABOUT THE PRESIDENT'S SAGGING SPIRITS!
R.N. CAN'T BE AN ACTIVIST PRESIDENT IF HE DOESN'T THINK HIS REMAINING TEAM IS STILL BEHIND HIM!
EVERYBODY READY?! LET'S MAKE THIS GOOD AND LOUD SO HE CAN HEAR IT UPSTAIRS!
GIVE ME AN "N"!
N!

GOOD NEWS, KIDDIES! TIME FOR ANOTHER EXCLUSIVE WBBY "WATERGATE PROFILE"! TODAY'S OBITUARY— JOHN MITCHELL!
JOHN MITCHELL, THE FORMER U.S. ATTORNEY-GENERAL, HAS IN RECENT WEEKS BEEN REPEATEDLY LINKED WITH BOTH THE WATERGATE CAPER AND ITS COVER-UP.
IT WOULD BE A DISSERVICE TO MR. MITCHELL AND HIS CHARACTER TO PREJUDGE THE MAN, BUT EVERYTHING KNOWN TO DATE COULD LEAD ONE TO CONCLUDE HE'S GUILTY!
GBTrudeau
THAT'S GUILTY! GUILTY, GUILTY, GUILTY!!

EHRLICHMAN? WHY ARE YOU PLANNING A PROFILE ON EHRLICHMAN? EVERYBODY ALREADY KNOWS WHO HE IS!
NOT SO, BERNIE! MAYBE YOU DO, BUT MOST FOLKS HAVEN'T ANY IDEA WHO HE IS OR WHAT HIS JOB WAS.
ALRIGHT, LOOK. HERE COMES MIKE. LET'S ASK HIM...
HI, GUYS, WHAT'S COOKIN'?
MIKE, DO YOU KNOW WHO JOHN EHRLICHMAN IS?
SECOND BASE FOR THE PADRES, RIGHT?
SEE?!
GBTrudeau

HOLY MOLY, CAMPERS! TIME FOR ANOTHER WBBY "WATERGATE PROFILE"! TODAY'S COVER-UP CUTIE IS... JOHN EHRLICHMAN!
"JOHN EHRLICHMAN, THE PRESIDENT'S ADVISOR ON DOMESTIC AFFAIRS, HAS FOR FOUR YEARS BEEN A CONSIDERABLE POWER IN THE WHITE HOUSE. YET UNTIL RECENTLY, MANY AMERICANS WERE UNAWARE OF THE SCOPE OF HIS DUTIES!
"ON THE AVERAGE DAY JOHN EHRLICHMAN USED TO CONSULT WITH MR. NIXON AT LEAST ONCE OR TWICE. IF THE WORD CAME DOWN HE WAS NEEDED, HE'D MAKE HIS WAY UP TO THE OVAL OFFICE WHERE HE WOULD INVARIABLY ENCOUNTER FELLOW STAFFER H.R. HALDEMAN!"
GB Trudeau
HALT! STOP OR I'LL SHOOT!
BOB! IT'S ME! IT'S ME!

HEEWACK! UN AUTRE "PROFILE" REQUEST! I'VE GOTTA HAND IT TO YOU, BOYS AND GIRLS — THERE'S BEEN TERRIFIC WATERGATE RESPONSE!
KEEP 'EM COMING, CAMPERS! GET THE FULL STORY — TRUTHS, INNUENDO, HEARSAY, THE WHOLE BIT — ON EVERYONE LINKED WITH THE NATION'S DARKEST SCANDAL!
FROM THE CUBAN BURGLARS TO THE CHIEF EXECUTIVE HIMSELF, IF YOU'VE GOT A FAVORITE WATERGATE CONSPIRATOR — AND YOU WANT TO KNOW MORE ABOUT HIM — REMEMBER TO PHONE IN YOUR REQUEST TO WBBY! THAT'S WBBY!!
OKAY! PROFILE OF JOHN DEAN III GOING OUT TO JOEY WITH HUGS FROM DONNA!
© BTrudeau

WELL, MOTHER O' MINE, IT'S TIME I LEFT FOR LAOS. I JUST GOT MY MARCHING ORDERS FROM THE PATHET LAO.
NOW YOU BE SURE TO WRITE ME IN... HEY! WHAT'S THIS?
©BTrudeau
IT'S A GOING-AWAY PRESENT! MOM, WHAT A THOUGHTFUL THING TO DO! HONESTLY...
"THE ALL-NEW TOMMY TOURIST GUIDE TO LAOS- 1961."
IT WAS ON SALE!

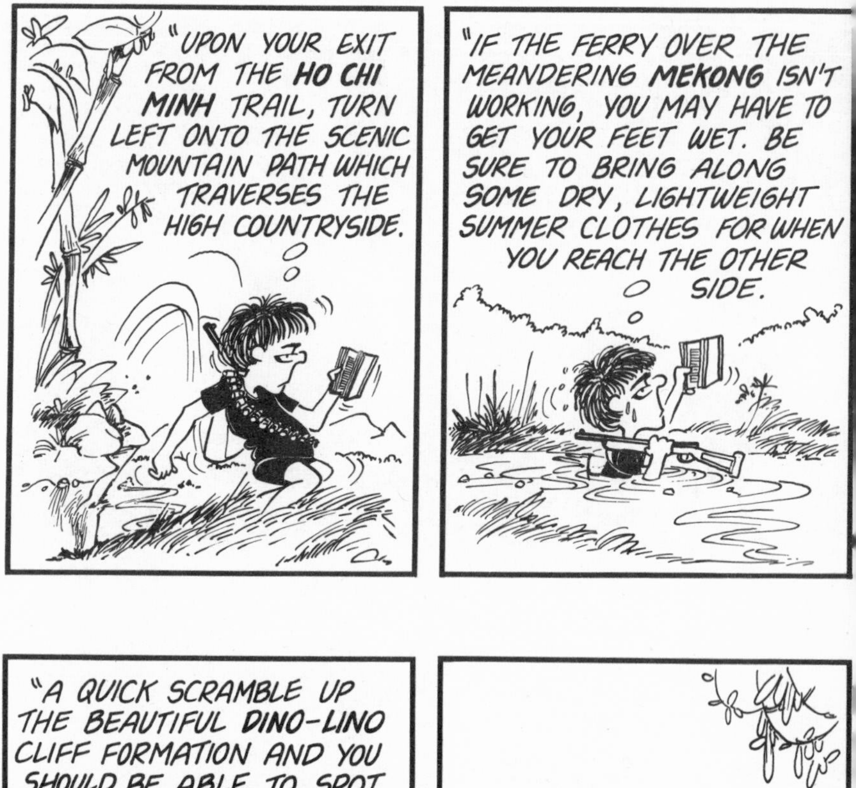
"UPON YOUR EXIT FROM THE HO CHI MINH TRAIL, TURN LEFT ONTO THE SCENIC MOUNTAIN PATH WHICH TRAVERSES THE HIGH COUNTRYSIDE.
"IF THE FERRY OVER THE MEANDERING MEKONG ISN'T WORKING, YOU MAY HAVE TO GET YOUR FEET WET. BE SURE TO BRING ALONG SOME DRY, LIGHTWEIGHT SUMMER CLOTHES FOR WHEN YOU REACH THE OTHER SIDE.
"A QUICK SCRAMBLE UP THE BEAUTIFUL DINO-LINO CLIFF FORMATION AND YOU SHOULD BE ABLE TO SPOT A SMALL LEDGE 80 YARDS ABOVE YOU. A SHORT, SPIRITED HIKE, AND THE TOURIST WILL SOON FIND HIMSELF AT THE TOP.
"WELCOME TO LAOS."
©BTrudeau

SIR?..
OH, SIR?..
PARDON US, SIR! WE ARE DESTITUTE, HUNGRY REFUGEES ON OUR WAY TO VIENTIANE! TAKE PITY ON US!
WE HAVE NOT EATEN IN DAYS! COULD NOT SOME OF US SHARE IN THE HOT RICE DINNER YOU HAVE PREPARED FOR YOURSELF?
UM..SURE. HOW MANY ARE THERE OF YOU?
135,000.
GBTrudeau

"ON YOUR LEFT, YOU SHOULD NOW SEE THE FAMOUS "JUMPING JARS INN." THIS QUAINT LITTLE RESTAURANT WITH ITS SIDEWALK TABLES HAS BEEN A FAVORITE WITH VISITORS FOR YEARS."
©BTrudeau
"BE SURE TO ASK FOR THE PROPRIETOR, 'LOO.' HE'LL BE DELIGHTED TO SERVE YOU ONE OF HIS TASTY, TANGY PUNCHES FOR WHICH HE IS RENOWNED THROUGHOUT THE PROVINCE."
"LOO"?
SORRY, MAN, WE'RE CLOSED.

AW, C'MON, LOO! CAN'T YOU EVEN FIX ME A LIGHT SNACK?
LOOK! I TOLD YOU! I'M CLOSED! I'VE BEEN BOMBED OUT OF BUSINESS!
LISTEN TO THIS, LOO: "WHILE THE LAOTIANS ARE A PROUD AND FIERCELY TENACIOUS PEOPLE, THEIR MOST OUT-STANDING CHARACTERISTIC IS GENEROSITY!
"WHETHER FOR A FRIEND IN NEED OR A PASSING STRANGER, THE LAOTIANS ARE ALWAYS QUICK ON THE DRAW WHEN IT COMES TO KINDNESS, COMPASSION, AND LENDING A HELPING HAND!
"FURTHERMORE..."
ALRIGHT ALREADY! I'LL TURN ON THE GRILL!
GBTrudeau

YESSIR! WE CERTAINLY HAVE BEEN EXPECTING YOU! I'LL HAVE EVERYTHING READY FOR YOU RIGHT AWAY!
CORPORAL! HE'S HERE! PREPARE A DINNER IMMEDIATELY! RIGHT! ALSO SEND OVER AN ORDERLY FOR HIS GEAR, AND ALERT THE C.O.!
HEE, HEE! THIS IS GREAT..
WILL YOU BE NEEDING ANYTHING ELSE, SIR?!
OH,..UM... YEAH! A HOT BATH AND A GOOD WOMAN!
HEAR THAT, CORPORAL? GET ON IT!
GBTrudeau

MY FELLOW COLLEAGUES! MUST I AGAIN IMPLORE THE SENATE TO PAY HEED TO THE WORSENING SITUATION IN SOUTHEAST ASIA? IS **CAMBODIA** TO BECOME **ANOTHER** VIETNAM?! IS...
HEY, GEORGE?..
WHAT? YOU'RE NOT LEAVING TOO, ARE YOU? DON'T YOU UNDERSTAND THIS IS **IMPORTANT**?
YEAH, GEORGE, I KNOW, BUT I PROMISED MY WIFE I'D TAKE HER TO DINNER. I'VE GOTTA GO!
WELL.. YES.. I SEE. GOOD NIGHT.
TURN OUT THE LIGHTS WHEN YOU FINISH, O.K.?
SIGH
©BTrudeau

WELL, HENRY?..
MR. PRESIDENT, I REALIZE THE SITUATION **IS** DETERIORATING OVER THERE, BUT I'M AFRAID ABSOLUTELY **NO ONE** ACCEPTS "PROTECTIVE REACTION" AS A CREDIBLE CONCEPT THESE DAYS.
HMM... WELL, WHAT ABOUT MY OTHER IDEA?
SIR?
"CAMBODIAZATION."
FORGET IT.
GBTrudeau

DAVID, YOUR RECENT BOOK, "THE BEST AND THE BRIGHTEST" HAS REALLY TAKEN OFF! HOW DO YOU EXPLAIN IT?
I THINK, MERV, THAT THE QUESTIONS OF THE VIETNAM QUAGMIRE HAVE LED MANY PEOPLE TO BECOME CURIOUS ABOUT THESE BRILLIANT JOHNSON AND KENNEDY AIDES WHO FIRST GOT US INVOLVED OVER THERE.
WELL, I WOULD THINK THAT WOULD BODE WELL FOR YOUR NEXT BOOK, DAVID. AS I UNDERSTAND IT, RECENT EVENTS HAVE INSPIRED YOU TO START WORK ON A HOT NEW SEQUEL!
THAT'S RIGHT, MERV. IT'S CALLED "THE WORST AND THE STUPIDEST."
OH? WHAT'S IT ABOUT?
©B Trudeau

WILL THERE BE ANYTHING ELSE THIS MORNING, MR. PRESIDENT?
NO, NO,.. I GUESS NOT, HAIG..
YOU SEEM A LITTLE DEPRESSED THIS MORNING, SIR..
SIGH.. I AM, OLD FRIEND, I AM...
HAIG.. YOU KNOW WHAT I NEED RIGHT NOW? I NEED SOMETHING TO BOOST MY MORALE, TO PICK UP MY SPIRITS...
GBTrudeau
HOW ABOUT IF I SEND OUT FOR SOME P.O.W.'S, SIR?
WHY... YES! THAT WOULD BE NICE!

GOOD MORNING, SENATOR. HAVE A NICE WEEKEND?
FABULOUS, MAXIE! IT WAS FILLED WITH BIRDIES AND PARS!
BUT I'M JUST AS GLAD TO BE BACK, FAITHFUL CONFIDANT – BACK TO REAFFIRM A STORMY LOVE AFFAIR WITH FEDERAL POLITICS!
GLORY! WHAT WITH ALL THE FRENETIC EXCITEMENT OF EXERCISING MY MANDATE, I'LL WAGER IT'LL SEEM LIKE NO TIME AT ALL BEFORE IT'S FRIDAY AFTERNOON AGAIN!
OF COURSE, IT IS WEDNESDAY ALREADY...
© BTrudeau

ONE FURTHER QUESTION, MR. COLSON...
WE HAVE HEARD PREVIOUS TESTIMONY TO THE EFFECT THAT YOU PROPOSED A BURGLARY AND FIRE-BOMBING OF THE BROOKINGS INSTITUTE IN 1971. WHAT SAY YOU?
OH NOW, SENATOR, THAT REMARK WASN'T MEANT TO BE TAKEN AS **SERIOUS**.. HEE-HEE.., OF COURSE NOT!... HOW RIDICULOUS!.. HOW **ABSURD**!
I WAS JUST BEING SILLY, SENATOR..
I'LL SAY.
©BTrudeau

WE INTERRUPT THE SENATE WATERGATE HEARINGS TO BRING YOU THIS SPECIAL BULLETIN.
TODAY ON THE PRE-EMPTED SOAP OPERA, "AS THE HOSPITAL TURNS," DR. HARDIN FINALLY DECIDED TO DIVORCE HIS WIFE RACHEL, AFTER FIVE YEARS OF MARRIAGE! A BITTER CUSTODY FIGHT IS EXPECTED.
TO REPEAT: DR. HARDIN IS GETTING A DIVORCE FROM RACHEL! THAT'S A FINAL.
©GBTrudeau
WE NOW RETURN TO OUR REGULARLY SCHEDULED BROADCAST.

THE CHAIR CALLS FOR THE NEXT WITNESS!
SENATOR, ALL THE WITNESSES FOR TODAY HAVE TESTIFIED.
BUT WE STILL HAVE TWO HOURS LEFT.
YESSIR, BUT NO OTHER WITNESSES ARE AVAILABLE.
HMM...
OKAY, THE CHAIR OPENS UP THE FLOOR TO INNUENDO AND HEARSAY.
ME FIRST!
NO, ME, ME!

MAXIE, MY LAD, I THINK I'VE FINALLY HIT ON A WAY TO BRING SOME REAL VIGOR TO THE HEARINGS!
THAT SO, BOSS?
YES, INDEED! RIDDLE ME THIS, YOUNG MAN: WHO ALONE HAS NEVER ONCE LOST THE TOTAL CONFIDENCE OF THE PRESIDENT?
BEATS ME.
HIS BRIDE! WE SHALL SUBPOENA THE FIRST LADY!
BUT OF COURSE! THINK SHE'LL COME?
NO WAY!
NOW, DICK, I THINK IT'D BE FUN..

HEAR THE GOOD NEWS, TOM? THE PRESIDENT IS APPEALING OUR SUBPOENA OF HIS WIFE! AT THE SUPREME COURT!
NO!
YES! BUT IT'S A FUTILE GESTURE. THE FIRST LADY WILL TESTIFY. I'M CERTAIN OF IT.
BUT WHAT DO YOU THINK SHE KNOWS, SENATOR?
CAN'T SAY FOR SURE. BUT IT'S ENTIRELY POSSIBLE THAT ONE NIGHT SHE OVERHEARD WHISPERS OF NAUGHTINESS WHILE TIPTOEING THROUGH THE HUSHED, CARPETED WHITE HOUSE CORRIDORS! YES! SOME MENTION OF A NASTINESS HITHERTO UNDISCLOSED!
HEE! HEE! HEE!
HEE, HEE! YOU'RE JUST AWFUL, SENATOR!
©BTrudeau

GOOD AFTERNOON. WELL, WE'VE BEEN CONFERRING LIKE CRAZY, AND I THINK WE HAVE GOT OURSELVES ANOTHER SNAPPY 5-4 DECISION.
THE SUPREME COURT OF THE UNITED STATES OF AMERICA HAS REVIEWED THE PRINCIPLE OF EXECUTIVE PRIVILEGE AS IT PERTAINS TO THE FIRST LADY. THE CONSENSUS IS THAT IT DOES NOT APPLY.
THE COURT THUS DIRECTS MRS. NIXON TO MAKE A SENATE HEARINGS APPEARANCE, INASMUCH AS IT FEELS SHE SHOULDN'T ENJOY THE IMMUNITY TO WHICH PRESIDENTIAL AIDES ARE CURRENTLY ENTITLED.
ALSO, THE COURT RATHER THINKS IT WOULD BE A GIGGLE.
Z Z Z
GBTrudeau

FRANKLY, MRS. NIXON, I FIND YOUR TESTIMONY INCREDIBLE! YOU STATE THAT YOU HAVE **NEVER** TALKED WITH **ANY** WHITE HOUSE AIDE! HOW CAN THAT BE?
MAY I ASK YOU A PERSONAL QUESTION, MRS. NIXON?
OF COURSE!
WHO **DO** YOU TALK TO IN THE WHITE HOUSE?
ONLY MY SECRET SERVICE AGENT AND MY PERSONAL HAIRDRESSER, FIFI.
NO FURTHER QUESTIONS.
THANK YOU-I'VE HAD A **LOVELY** TIME!
©GBTrudeau

LEONARD, AS MY COUNSEL, I THINK IT'S ABOUT TIME YOU TOOK A LOOK AT THESE TRANSCRIPTS OF THE SECRET TAPES...
AS YOU CAN SEE, THERE ARE MANY FRANK AND CANDID REMARKS WHICH, IF TAKEN OUT OF CONTEXT, MIGHT CREATE A FALSE IMPRESSION.
YESSIR. I CAN SEE ONE HERE ON PAGE TWO.
WHICH ONE'S THAT?
"WELL, JOHN, HOW'S THE COVER-UP GOING?"
RIGHT! A GOOD EXAMPLE!
YESSIR. IT **COULD** BE MISINTERPRETED.
GBTrudeau

YES, WHAT IS IT, MEL?
SIR, WE'VE BEEN GETTING A LOT MORE HEAT FROM CONGRESS OVER THE TAPES. PERHAPS WE SHOULD RECONSIDER..
GO AWAY, MEL. I'M MINDING THE PEOPLE'S BUSINESS.
BUT, SIR, EVEN THE LOYALIST SENATORS ARE NOW INSISTING THE PEOPLE HAVE THE RIGHT TO KNOW.
THE SENATORS ARE NOT IN A POSITION TO INSIST.
AND THE PEOPLE?
THEY SHOULD MIND THEIR OWN BUSINESS.
GBTrudeau

GOOD EVENING. WELCOME TO ABC NEWS!
HARRY'S ON VACATION, AND HOWARD'S ON ASSIGNMENT. FRANK IS ON THE ROAD.
SAM IS OFF THE AIR, TOM IS IN TRANSIT, AND TINA IS OUT TO LUNCH. I'M THE ONLY ONE LEFT HERE. MY NAME IS CARLOS; I WORK UPSTAIRS IN THE STOCK-ROOM.
HERE ARE TONIGHT'S HEADLINES..

BUT CONGRESSMAN, YOU HAVE TO VIEW THE SECRET CAMBODIAN BOMBINGS IN PERSPECTIVE, IN THE PROPER TIME-FRAME!
TIME-FRAME, GENERAL?
YES, SIR.. YOU SEE, THERE WERE DOZENS OF BOMBINGS ON CAMPUSES ALL ACROSS THE COUNTRY..
NATURALLY, THAT KIND OF ATMOSPHERE LED A FEW WELL-INTENTIONED BUT OVERZEALOUS OFFICIALS TO BELIEVE THAT BOMBING WAS AN ACCEPTABLE MEANS OF SOCIAL CHANGE.
OH, **THAT** TIME-FRAME!
YES, SIR.
GBTrudeau

WHAT IS IT, HAIG?
SIR, IT'S ABOUT THE HOUSE HEARINGS ON THE SECRET CAMBODIAN BOMBINGS...
WE NEED TO KNOW MORE ABOUT THE RAIDS, SIR. THEY SAY NOBODY BUT YOU KNEW ABOUT THEM.
IT'S NOT TRUE! I TOLD EVERYBODY WHO HAD A NEED OR RIGHT TO KNOW!
YES, SIR, BUT WHO? YOU'VE GOT TO BE MORE SPECIFIC.
WELL, LET ME SEE... THE PILOTS, OF COURSE...
YES, GO ON...
GBTrudeau

JOANIE, I WONDER IF YOU'D BREAK YOUR DATING MORATORIUM AND GO OUT WITH ME TONIGHT..
THANKS, SCOT, BUT I'D REALLY RATHER NOT...
GEE, I THINK YOU'LL REGRET IT, JOANIE. I REALLY DO..
WHAT DO YOU MEAN, SCOT?
WELL, YOU SEE, I JUST HAPPEN TO HAVE TWO TICKETS TO THE JEB MAGRUDER CONCERT..
©GBTrudeau
SCOT! HONEY!
HEE, HEE... AT WHAT POINT IN TIME SHALL I PICK YOU UP?

SCOTTY, HOW DID YOU EVER GET SUCH GREAT SEATS FOR JEB MAGRUDER'S CONCERT?
IT WASN'T EASY, JOANIE!
YOU KNOW, JEB'S MY FAVORITE CONSPIRATOR! I DON'T KNOW WHY - MAYBE IT'S HIS BOYISH GOOD LOOKS!
WHAT'S ON THE PROGRAM FOR TONIGHT?
LEMME SEE.. THE FIRST ACT IS EXCERPTS FROM HIS DIARY. AFTER THAT THERE'S A COVER-UP SYNOPSIS, FOLLOWED BY A QUESTION-AND-ANSWER PERIOD.
THE LAST ACT IS HIS PLEA FOR FORGIVENESS AND UNDER-STANDING.
OH, I HEAR THAT'S GREAT!

LADIES AND GENTLEMEN!... MR. JEB MAGRUDER!
CLAP!
CLAP!
YEA!
YEA!
YEA!
CLAP!
CLAP!
CLAP!
CLAP!
CLAP!
YEA!
CLAP!
WELL, LET ME HEAR YA SAY YEAH!
YEAH!
YEAH!
CLAP!
CLAP!
CLAP!
© GBTrudeau

MR. MAGRUDER, ARE YOU GLAD YOU'VE COME CLEAN?
OF COURSE! I'LL NEVER FORGET THE MOMENT WHEN I REALIZED THAT WATERGATE WAS **WRONG**! IT WAS... BEAUTIFUL.
YEA, THE SCALES FELL FROM MY EYES, AND I SAW WATERGATE FOR THE **INSIDIOUS, UGLY MONSTER** IT REALLY WAS!!
WHEN WAS THAT?
TO THE BEST OF MY RECOLLECTION, ABOUT MID-JUNE.

IN CONCLUSION, LET US ALL REMEMBER– TO ERR IS HUMAN, TO FORGIVE IS DIVINE!
FORGIVE ME, AMERICA!
WE FORGIVE YOU, JEB!
TOP THAT, MR. SECRET TAPES.
YEA! YEA!
YEA! YEA!
CLAP! CLAP!
CLAP! CLAP!

XIT
WELL, LOOK, MICK, JUST LOAD UP THE AMPS, AND I'LL GET TOM TO DO THE REST..
O.K.
JEB
WBBY
XIT
CAN I HELP YOU?
YES, I'M FROM THE CAMPUS RADIO, MR. MAGRUDER. I WONDER IF YOU COULD TELL ME WHAT YOUR PLANS ARE..
WBBY
WELL, I'VE GOT A GIG AT AUBURN NEXT WEEK, THEN THE UNIVERSITY OF ILLINOIS, AND THEN A BENEFIT CONCERT IN L.A..
BENEFIT CONCERT? FOR WHOM?
WBBY
XIT
DUNNO YET... PROBABLY AN EARTHQUAKE FUND OR SOMETHING...
WBBY

BZZZ!
RING!
RING! RING!
RING!
BRRR!
RING!
JONES HERE.
YES?
HELLO?
WHAT IS IT?
YEAH?
YESSIR! RIGHT AWAY!
FINE! SEND HIM IN!
LET ME CHECK..
RIGHT!
VERY GOOD! I'LL GET ON IT!
AAAHH.. THE PEOPLE'S BUSINESS!
GBTrudeau

ARE YOU SURE YOU WANT TO GO THROUGH WITH THIS PRESS CONFERENCE, SIR? IT WILL JUST BE ANOTHER BARRAGE OF WATERGATE QUESTIONS.
NONSENSE! THEY'LL WANT TO KNOW ABOUT THE MID-EAST, WHY I HAVE TAKEN THE BOLD AND DECISIVE ACTION OF PUTTING OUR TROOPS ON WORLD-WIDE MILITARY ALERT!
BUT SIR, THE TROOPS AREN'T ON A WORLD-WIDE MILITARY ALERT.
THEY'RE NOT? BUT.. BUT.. THIS MORNING I GAVE DIRECT ORDERS...
HAIG!
OH, GEE, I'M SORRY, SIR, I FORGOT...
© G B Trudeau

TODAY AT A PRESS CONFERENCE, THE PRESIDENT LASHED OUT AT THE TELEVISION MEDIA FOR WHAT HE CALLED BIASED COVERAGE OF THE WATERGATE AFFAIR.
SAID MR. NIXON, "IN ALL MY YEARS OF POLITICS, NEVER HAVE I SEEN SUCH OUTRAGEOUS, VICIOUS, DISTORTED, AND ERRONEOUS REPORTING!"
HE WENT ON TO CONDEMN TELEVISION COMMENTATORS FOR "THE VINDICTIVE LEERS AND SNEERS DIRECTED AT THE GREAT OFFICE OF THE PRESIDENCY."
MOST REPORTERS PRESENT AGREED THE PRESIDENT WAS BEING HIS USUAL, ASININE SELF.
©B Trudeau

TED, MR. SMITH HERE IS WORKING FOR THE SPECIAL PROSECUTOR. HE'D LIKE TO HEAR THE TAPE OF LAST APRIL 9.
YESSIR, MR. PRESIDENT!
WE'LL HAVE IT FOR YOU IN A MINUTE, MR. SMITH. AS YOU KNOW, I AND MY STAFF ARE **EAGER** TO HELP THE SPECIAL PROSECUTOR'S OFFICE IN **ANY** WAY WE CAN!
WELL, TED?
GOSH, MR. PRESIDENT! AS LUCK WOULD HAVE IT, **BOTH** RECORDING MACHINES WERE OUT BEING REPAIRED THAT DAY!
HOLY **SMOKES**! WHAT A COINCIDENCE!
GBTrudeau

WHAT DO YOU WANT MOST FOR CHRISTMAS, DADDY?
THINGS YOU CAN'T GIVE ME, TRICIA. THINGS LIKE MY OLD MANDATE, AND DÉTENTE, VINDICATION, AND A GENERATION OF PEACE.
WOULD YOU SETTLE FOR A DAY OF PEACE, AND THE LOVE OF YOUR FAMILY?
HEE, HEE.. YOU **KNOW** I WOULD, PRINCESS.
MERRY CHRISTMAS, DADDY!
GBTrudeau